Animals That Live in the Mountains/
Animales de las montañas

Golden Eagles/
Águilas reales

By JoAnn Early Macken

Reading Consultant: Jeanne Clidas, Ph.D.
Director, Roberts Wesleyan College Literacy Clinic

WEEKLY READER®
PUBLISHING

APR   2012

Please visit our web site at **www.garethstevens.com**.
For a free catalog describing our list of high-quality books,
call 1-877-542-2595 (USA) or 1-800-387-3178 (Canada).
Our fax: 1-877-542-2596

Library of Congress Cataloging-in-Publication Data

Macken, JoAnn Early, 1953–
    [Golden eagles. Spanish & English]
    Golden eagles = Águilas reales / by JoAnn Early Macken.
      p. cm. — (Animals that live in the mountains = Animales de las montañas)
    Includes bibliographical references and index.
    ISBN-10: 1-4339-2445-5   ISBN-13: 978-1-4339-2445-3 (lib. bdg.)
    ISBN-10: 1-4339-2503-6   ISBN-13: 978-1-4339-2503-0 (soft cover)
    1. Golden eagle—Juvenile literature. I. Title. II. Title: Águilas reales.
  QL696.F32M253 2010
  98.9'42—dc22
                                        2009007410

This edition first published in 2010 by
Weekly Reader® Books
An Imprint of Gareth Stevens Publishing
1 Reader's Digest Road
Pleasantville, NY 10570-7000 USA

Executive Managing Editor: Lisa M. Herrington
Senior Editor: Barbara Bakowski
Cover Designers: Jennifer Ryder-Talbot and Studio Montage
Production: Studio Montage
Translators: Tatiana Acosta and Guillermo Gutiérrez
Library Consultant: Carl Harvey, Library Media Specialist, Noblesville, Indiana

Photo credits: Cover, pp. 1, 9, 11, 19 Shutterstock; pp. 5, 13, 17 © Tom and Pat Leeson;
p. 7 © Yuri Shibnev/naturepl.com; p. 15 Digital Stock; p. 21 © Alan and Sandy Carey

Printed in the United States of America

Table of Contents

- - - - - - - - - - -

Contenido

Boldface words appear in the glossary./
Las palabras en **negrita** aparecen en el glosario.

Baby Eagles

Golden eagles build huge nests. Each year, they add more sticks. Baby eagles are called **eaglets**. They hatch in the nests.

- - - - - - - - - - - - - -

Crías de águila

Las águilas reales hacen nidos enormes. Cada año añaden nuevos palitos. Las crías de águila se llaman aguiluchos. Los **aguiluchos** salen del huevo en el nido.

eaglet/
aguilucho

An eaglet has soft feathers called **down**.
Its father brings it meat to eat. Its mother
feeds it small pieces.

- - - - - - - - - - - - - -

Un aguilucho tiene unas plumas suaves
llamadas **plumón**. Su padre trae carne
para alimentarlo. Su madre se la va dando
en pequeños trozos.

down/
plumón

Feathers and Flying

Eagles start to fly in about three months. They fly and hunt during the day. At night, they rest in trees.

- - - - - - - - - - - - - -

Plumas y vuelo

Las águilas comienzan a volar, más o menos, a los tres meses. Durante el día, vuelan y cazan. Por la noche, descansan en los árboles.

Golden eagles have gold feathers on their heads and necks. Feathers cover their legs.

- - - - - - - - - - - - - - -

Las águilas reales tienen plumas doradas en la cabeza y el cuello. Sus patas están cubiertas de plumas.

legs/
patas

A golden eagle can hear well. It listens for other eagles. It listens for storms. If an eagle gets wet, it may not be able to fly.

— — — — — — — — — — — — — —

El águila real puede oír muy bien. Oye a otras águilas. Oye la llegada de una tormenta. Si un águila se moja, podría tener problemas para volar.

Strong Hunters

A golden eagle may fly many miles to find food. It can spot **prey** from far away.

- - - - - - - - - - - - - -

Grandes cazadoras

Un águila real puede llegar a volar muchas millas en busca de comida. Es capaz de ver a una **presa** desde muy lejos.

Eagles dive from the sky. They catch their prey with claws called **talons**.

- - - - - - - - - - - - - -

Las águilas descienden en picado desde el cielo. Atrapan a sus presas con las uñas, o **garras**.

talons/
garras

Eagles have strong hooked **beaks**. They tear their prey apart. Golden eagles hunt rabbits and mice. They also eat lizards and birds.

- - - - - - - - - - - - - - -

Las águilas tienen **picos** ganchudos y fuertes. Despedazan a sus presas. Las águilas reales cazan conejos y ratones. También comen lagartos y aves.

beak/
pico

In winter, golden eagles may fly to warmer places to find food. They follow their prey down the mountains. In spring, the eagles fly back up.

En el invierno, las águilas reales pueden volar a lugares más cálidos en busca de comida. Siguen a sus presas a zonas más bajas. En la primavera, las águilas reales regresan a las montañas.

Fast Facts/Datos básicos

Height/ Altura	about 3 feet (1 meter)/ unos 3 pies (1 metro)
Wingspan/ Envergadura	about 7 feet (2 meters)/ unos 7 pies (2 metros)
Weight/ Peso	about 15 pounds (7 kilograms)/ unas 15 libras (7 kilogramos)
Diet/ Dieta	birds and other small animals/aves y otros animales pequeños
Average life span/ Promedio de vida	up to 20 years/ hasta 20 años

Glossary/Glosario

beaks: the bills of birds

down: soft, fluffy feathers

eaglets: baby eagles

prey: animals that are killed for food

talons: claws

- - - - - - - - - - - - - - - - - -

aguiluchos: crías de águila

garras: uñas afiladas

picos: partes de la cabeza de las aves

plumón: plumas suaves y mullidas

presa: animal devorado por otro animal

For More Information/Más información

Books/Libros

Eagles. New Naturebooks (series). Patrick Merrick (Child's World, 2006)

I Live in the Mountains/Vivo en las montañas. Where I Live (series). Gini Holland (Gareth Stevens, 2004)

Web Sites/Páginas web

Golden Eagle/Águilas reales

www.birds.cornell.edu/AllAboutBirds/BirdGuide/Golden_Eagle_dtl.html
Listen to sound files of an eagle's call./Escuchen cómo suena la llamada de un águila.

Golden Eagle/Águilas reales

www.baldeagleinfo.com/eagle/eagle7.html
Watch a video of a golden eagle./Vean un video de un águila real.

Index/Índice

About the Author

JoAnn Early Macken is the author of two rhyming picture books, *Sing-Along Song* and *Cats on Judy*, and more than 80 nonfiction books for children. Her poems have appeared in several children's magazines. She lives in Wisconsin with her husband and their two sons.

- - - - - - - - - - - - - - - -

Información sobre la autora

JoAnn Early Macken ha escrito dos libros de rimas con ilustraciones, *Sing-Along Song* y *Cats on Judy*, y más de ochenta libros de no ficción para niños. Sus poemas han sido publicados en varias revistas infantiles. Vive en Wisconsin con su esposo y sus dos hijos.